Weight Watchers™

D0416644

Fast and Fabulous

LOUISE TYLER

SIMON & SCHUSTER

A VIACOM COMPANY

First published in Great Britain by Simon & Schuster, 1998
A Viacom Company

Simon & Schuster Ltd
West Garden Place
Kendal Street
London W2 2AQ

Design: Moore Lowenhoff
Cover design: Jane Humphrey
Typesetting: Stylize
Photography: Steve Baxter
Styling: Marian Price
Food preparation: Sara Buenfeld

Weight Watchers Publications Manager: Juliet Hudson
Weight Watchers Publications Assistant: Celia Whiston

A CIP catalogue record is available from the British Library

ISBN 0 68481 977 5

Printed and bound in Belgium

Pictured on the front cover: *Pork with Mushroom, Mustard and Tarragon Sauce (page 55)*

Pictured on the back cover: *Baked Bananas (page 60)* and *Stewed Prunes with Brandy (page 60)*

Recipe notes:
Egg size is medium, unless otherwise stated.
Vegetables are medium-sized, unless otherwise stated.
It is important to use proper measuring spoons, not cutlery, for spoon measures.
1 tablespoon = 15 ml; 1 teaspoon = 5 ml.
Dried herbs can be substituted for fresh ones, but the flavour may not always
be as good. Halve the fresh herb quantity stated in the recipe.

Contents

Introduction

Losing weight doesn't mean that you have to starve or make yourself miserable, and, as these recipes prove, cutting down on fat certainly doesn't mean compromising on taste.

Here you'll find over 70 recipes for dishes which are both delicious and satisfying. Who would have thought it was possible to enjoy 'Chicken with a Herb and Parmesan Crust', 'Mocha 'n' Orange Mousse' or even 'Blackberry and Apple Cake' on a diet? And each recipe gives the Calories per serving and Points per serving, so working out your daily menu couldn't be easier.

Weight Watchers *1,2,3 Success Plus*™ means that dieting will never be the same again and meal-times will be a pleasure for you and all the family too. You will learn to choose foods which are low in Points so that you can get the most from your daily allowance and in turn be eating in a more healthy way.

Many of these recipes use fresh herbs. Their flavour is so much better than that of dried herbs: they can transform a dish from good to fabulous so try to use them as much as you can. Happily, fresh herbs are readily available now in the supermarkets in the fruit and vegetable department and you can either buy them packaged or in pots which you can put on the windowsill. If you want, you can even grow your own herbs and have them on hand when you need them.

Soups and Starters

These warming soups and tasty starters are wonderful ways to start a meal; they're also quick and easy and low in Points so you won't waste too much time in the kitchen or use up too many Points. They can also become a meal in themselves if you serve them with plenty of salad and some bread.

Parsnip and Apple Soup

Serves 4

Preparation and cooking time:
35 minutes
Calories per serving: 90

Freezing: recommended

Ⓥ

Comforting and delicious, this soup is ideal on a cold wintery day.

1 teaspoon olive oil, corn oil or sunflower oil
1 onion, chopped
4 parsnips, peeled and chopped
1 Bramley apple, peeled, cored and chopped
2 teaspoons chopped fresh thyme, or 1 teaspoon dried
600 ml (1 pint) vegetable stock
4 tablespoons half-fat crème fraîche
salt and freshly ground black pepper

1. Heat the oil in a medium saucepan. Add the onion, parsnips, apple and thyme and fry for 4–5 minutes, until beginning to soften.
2. Add the stock, bring to the boil and cover and simmer for 20–25 minutes, or until the parsnips are tender.
3. Transfer the soup to a blender or food processor and process until smooth. Return to the pan and stir through the crème fraîche. Season, heat through (but do not boil) and serve.

Points per serving: 2
Total Points per recipe: 8

Provençale Fish Soup with Gruyère Toasts

Serves 4

Preparation and cooking time:
40 minutes
Calories per serving: 190

Freezing: not recommended

For the soup:
1 teaspoon olive oil, corn oil or sunflower oil
1 leek, halved lengthways and sliced
1 onion, chopped
1 garlic clove, crushed
1 large potato, diced
1 red pepper, de-seeded and chopped

450 ml (16 fl oz) fish stock
400 g can of chopped tomatoes
1 teaspoon herbes de Provence or dried mixed herbs
300 g (10½ oz) skinless, boneless cod or haddock, cubed
175 g (6 oz) cooked, peeled prawns
salt and freshly ground black pepper
For the Gruyère toasts:
25 g (1 oz) Gruyère cheese, grated finely
8 slices of french bread (each 2.5 cm/1 inch thick), toasted on one side

1. Preheat the grill.
2. Heat the oil in a medium saucepan. Add the leek, onion, garlic, potato and red pepper and fry for 4–5 minutes or until beginning to soften.
3. Add the stock, tomatoes and herbs to the pan. Bring to the boil, cover and simmer for 15–20 minutes.
4. Transfer half the soup mixture to a blender or food processor and process until smooth.
5. Return the puréed soup to the pan along with the fish, season well, cover and simmer for 5–7 minutes or until the fish is cooked, adding the prawns 2 minutes before the end of the cooking time.
6. Meanwhile, sprinkle the Gruyère cheese on the untoasted side of bread and place under the grill for 1–2 minutes or until melted and bubbling. Serve with the soup.

Points per serving: 7
Total Points per recipe: 28

Variation:
Points per serving without the Gruyère toasts are 5.

Icy Summer Gazpacho

Serves 4

Preparation time: 10 minutes
+ at least 1 hour chilling
Calories per serving: 100

Freezing: not recommended

(V)

**Serve this delicious soup on
a hot summer evening with
fresh crusty bread.**

750 g (1 lb 10 oz) plum
  tomatoes, skinned, de-seeded
  and chopped
1 green pepper, de-seeded and
  chopped
1 cucumber, chopped
1 celery stick, chopped
10 fresh basil leaves, torn
600 ml (1 pint) tomato juice or
  passata
2 tablespoons red wine vinegar
2 garlic cloves, crushed
1 red chilli, chopped finely
2 medium slices of white bread,
  crusts removed
salt and freshly ground black
  pepper
To serve:
ice cubes
fresh basil leaves

1. Place the tomatoes, green pepper and cucumber in a bowl.
2. Place the remaining ingredients in a blender or food processor
and blend until smooth. Add to the vegetables and chill for at least
1 hour.
3. Serve topped with the ice cubes and basil.

Points per serving: 1
Total Points per recipe: 4

Cook's note:
Remove the seeds from the chilli if you prefer a less fiery taste.
You can also substitute fresh ordinary tomatoes for plum tomatoes
since they are less expensive.

Mixed Bean and Lentil Soup

Serves 4

Preparation time: 15 minutes
Cooking time: 25 minutes
Calories per serving: 135

Freezing: not recommended

(V)

**This warming soup is delicious
with a spoonful of tasty pesto.**

1 teaspoon olive oil, corn oil or
  sunflower oil
1 leek, sliced
1 garlic clove, crushed
2 celery sticks, sliced
2 teaspoons chopped fresh
  thyme or 1 teaspoon dried
700 ml (1¼ pints) vegetable
  stock
25 g (1 oz) dried green lentils
50 g (1¾ oz) french beans,
  halved
425 g can of flageolet beans,
  drained and rinsed
25 g (1 oz) frozen peas
4 teaspoons green pesto
salt and freshly ground black
  pepper

1. Heat the oil in a medium saucepan. Add the leek, garlic, celery
and thyme and fry for 3–4 minutes until beginning to soften.
2. Add the stock and lentils and bring to the boil. Cover and
simmer for 25 minutes, adding the french beans, flageolet beans
and the peas 5 minutes before the end of the cooking time.
3. Season well. Transfer to serving dishes and top with a teaspoon
of pesto.

Points per serving: 2½
Total Points per recipe: 10

Chicken Satay with Chilli Dipping Sauce

Serves 4

Preparation and cooking time:
15 minutes + 30 minutes
marinating
Calories per serving: 170

Freezing: not recommended

Grilled chicken is perfect with
this sweet chilli sauce.

For the satay:
25 g (1 oz) creamed coconut,
    dissolved in 4 tablespoons
    boiling water
1 garlic clove, crushed
2 teaspoons soft brown sugar
1/2 teaspoon turmeric
1/2 teaspoon ground cumin
1/2 teaspoon ground coriander
2 medium boneless, skinless
    chicken breasts (approximately
    150 g/51/2 oz each), sliced
    thinly
For the sweet chilli sauce:
2 tablespoons chilli sauce
2 tablespoons runny honey
2 tablespoons fresh coriander,
    chopped

1. Preheat the grill.
2. In a non-metallic bowl, mix together the coconut mixture, garlic,
sugar and spices. Add the chicken, coating it with the spice mixture
and leave to marinate for at least 30 minutes.
3. Make the chilli dipping sauce by combining all the ingredients
together in a bowl.
4. Thread the chicken onto 8 wooden skewers and cook under a
preheated grill for 5–6 minutes, or until cooked, turning
occasionally. Serve with the chilli sauce.

Points per serving: 31/2
Total Points per recipe: 14

Cook's note:
Soak the wooden skewers in a bowl of water for at least 10 minutes
before threading on the chicken. This will help to prevent the
skewers from burning and breaking when grilled.

Variation:
Substitute pork, beef or tiger prawns for the chicken. There will be
41/2 Points per serving with pork or beef and 31/2 Points per serving
with prawns.

Tomato and Mozzarella Bruschetta

Serves 4

Preparation and cooking time:
10 minutes
Calories per serving: 145

Freezing: not recommended

Ⓥ

In Italy, bruschetta are a
popular choice as a snack or
starter.

1 small french stick, cut into
    8 slices (approximately
    2.5 cm/1 inch thick)
1 garlic clove
2 plum tomatoes, cut into
    chunks
50 g (13/4 oz) half-fat mozzarella
a handful of fresh basil
1 tablespoon balsamic vinegar
1 tablespoon olive oil
salt and freshly ground black
    pepper

1. Toast the bread on each side. Rub each side of the bread with
the garlic.
2. Top with the tomatoes and mozzarella and basil and then drizzle
over the vinegar and oil. Season well and serve immediately.

Points per serving: 3
Total Points per recipe: 12

Variations:
Feel free to try a variety of different toppings such as pesto, roasted
peppers, olives, marinated artichoke hearts, parma ham, anchovies,
sun-dried tomatoes, asparagus or parmesan shavings. Just remember
to count the Points.

Goat's Cheese and Tomato Tartlets

Serves 4

Preparation and cooking time:
25 minutes
Calories per serving: 110

Freezing: not recommended

ⓥ if using vegetarian goat's
cheese

Goat's cheese, oregano and
tomato are a heavenly
combination of flavours.

4 filo pastry sheets (25 cm/
  10 inches square)
1 tablespoon olive oil
16 cherry tomatoes, halved
100 g (3½ oz) firm goat's
  cheese, cut into 4 slices
2 teaspoons chopped fresh
  oregano or 1 teaspoon dried
salt and freshly ground black
  pepper

1. Preheat the oven to Gas Mark 6/200°C/400°F.
2. Brush each piece of filo with a little of the olive oil, then cut into
   quarters. Line 4 (8 cm/3-inch) loose-bottomed flan tins with 4
   squares of the pastry each, then brush with the remaining oil.
3. Place half of the tomatoes in the bottom of the tarts, cover each
   with a slice of cheese and then top with the remaining tomatoes.
4. Sprinkle over the oregano and season well.
5. Cook for 10–12 minutes or until the pastry is golden and the
   cheese has begun to melt. Serve immediately.

Points per serving: 3
Total Points per recipe: 12

Cook's note:
If you prefer, you could use Camembert or Brie instead of the goat's
cheese. The Points will be 4 per serving.

Prawns in a Spicy Tomato Sauce

Serves 4

Preparation and cooking time:
25 minutes
Calories per serving: 110

Freezing: not recommended

Freshly grilled prawns are
wonderful with a light spicy
sauce.

12–16 raw king prawns,
  defrosted if frozen
2 teaspoons olive oil, corn oil
  or sunflower oil
1 small onion, chopped
2 garlic cloves, crushed
1 teaspoon black mustard seeds
¼ teaspoon dried chilli flakes
1 red pepper, de-seeded and
  chopped
3 ripe tomatoes, skinned and
  chopped
4 tablespoons dry white wine
  or stock
2 tablespoons unsalted cashew
  nuts, toasted and chopped
2 tablespoons chopped fresh
  coriander
salt and freshly ground black
  pepper

1. Shell the prawns, then make a slit down the back of each and
remove the black intestine.
2. Heat 1 teaspoon of the oil in a saucepan and add the onion, garlic,
mustard seeds, chilli flakes and red pepper. Fry for 3–4 minutes or
until the onion and pepper begin to soften.
3. Add the tomatoes and wine or stock and bring to the boil. Cover
and simmer for 10 minutes. Transfer to a blender or food processor
and process until smooth. Season to taste.
4. Meanwhile, place the prawns on a baking tray, brush with the
remaining oil and cook under a preheated grill for 3–4 minutes or
until cooked through.
5. Serve the prawns with the sauce and top with the nuts and
coriander.

Points per serving: 2
Total Points per recipe: 8

Variations:
King prawns can be expensive. For a cheaper version of this recipe,
use 250 g (9 oz) cooked and peeled small prawns. Simply stir them
through the sauce until hot and serve with the nuts and coriander.
Add ½ Point per serving.

Garlic Mushrooms

Serves 4

Preparation and cooking time: 10 minutes
Calories per serving: 60

Freezing: not recommended

Ⓥ

8 large flat-cap mushrooms
2 garlic cloves, chopped finely
6 tablespoons vegetable stock
8 slices of french bread (each 2.5 cm/1 inch thick), toasted
2 tablespoons chopped fresh parsley
salt and freshly ground black pepper

These tasty garlic mushrooms are made without using any fat. Once you've tried these, there'll be no turning back.

1. Place the mushrooms (gills upwards) in a frying-pan. Sprinkle over the garlic and pour over the stock.
2. Cover the pan and simmer for 4–5 minutes until the mushrooms are cooked. Season well.
3. Place the mushrooms on the french toasts, pour over the cooking juices and sprinkle with the parsley.

Points per serving: 1½
Total Points per recipe: 6

Baked Sweetcorn with Mint Dip

Serves 4

Preparation time: 10 minutes
Cooking time: 20 minutes
Calories per serving: 115

Freezing: not recommended

Ⓥ

Baking corn on the cob in foil greatly enhances the flavour.

4 medium corn on the cob, husks removed
For the mint dip:
150 g (5½ oz) carton of low-fat natural yogurt
2 tablespoons chopped fresh mint
2 tablespoons chopped fresh parsley
1 garlic clove, crushed
a few drops of Tabasco sauce
salt and freshly ground black pepper

1. Preheat the oven to Gas Mark 6/200°C/400°F.
2. Wrap each cob in a piece of foil. Cook in the oven for 15–20 minutes or until the kernels are tender.
3. Make the sauce by mixing together all the ingredients and then season to taste. Serve as a dipping sauce with the corn on the cob.

Points per serving: 1½
Total Points per recipe: 6

Cook's note:
Corn on the cob are also ideal for the barbecue.

Suppers and Snacks

Tired of the same old sandwiches and beans on toast? Well, here are some fabulous new ideas for snacks or light meals. If you fancy Mexican, you can whip up Vegetable Enchiladas and smother them with tasty guacamole; if you're craving pizza, try the seafood version here. And if you want to enjoy an old favourite with a difference, try the Stuffed Baked Potato with mustard, spring onions and cream cheese.

Chicken Liver Salad with Garlic Croûtons

Serves 2

Preparation and cooking time: 10 minutes
Calories per serving: 185

Freezing: not recommended

Chicken livers are economical and full of iron and a tasty ingredient for salad.

1 teaspoon olive oil, corn oil or sunflower oil
150 g (5½ oz) chicken livers, trimmed and halved
2 teaspoons grainy mustard
2 tablespoons balsamic vinegar
60 g bag of mixed lettuce leaves
2 spring onions, sliced
For the croûtons:
4 medium slices of ciabatta or french bread (each 2.5 cm/ 1 inch thick), toasted
1 garlic clove

1. Heat the oil in a non-stick frying-pan, add the chicken livers and then fry for 2–3 minutes until browned on the outside, but still retaining some pink in the middle. Remove from the heat and stir in the mustard and vinegar.
2. Divide the lettuce leaves and spring onions between 2 serving plates.
3. Rub one side of the toasts with the garlic, discard the garlic and place the toasts on plates. Spoon over the chicken livers and pan juices and serve immediately.

Points per serving: 4½
Total Points per recipe: 9

Cook's note:
Chicken livers are usually found in the freezer section in supermarkets. Make sure that they are thoroughly defrosted before cooking.

Vegetable Enchiladas with Guacamole

Serves 4

Preparation and cooking time: 25 minutes
Calories per serving: 345

Freezing: not recommended

(V) if using vegetarian Cheddar

A Mexican favourite and just another excuse to enjoy the wonderful taste of guacamole.

1 teaspoon oil
2 onions, sliced
1 red pepper, de-seeded and sliced

1 green pepper, de-seeded and sliced
150 g (5½ oz) baby sweetcorn, halved lengthways
1 large courgette, cut into strips
8 medium flour tortillas
40 g (1½ oz) mature Cheddar, grated
For the guacamole:
1 medium ripe avocado, mashed
juice of half a lemon
2 tomatoes, chopped finely
1 teaspoon sweet chilli sauce
2 tablespoons chopped fresh coriander

1. Heat the oil in a large frying-pan or wok. Add the onions, peppers, baby sweetcorn and courgette. Stir-fry for 4–5 minutes, or until beginning to soften and brown in places.
2. Make the guacamole by mixing together all the ingredients in a non-metallic bowl.
3. Warm the tortillas according to the packet instructions.
4. To serve, divide the stir-fried vegetables between the tortillas, sprinkle over the cheese, roll up and serve with the guacamole.

Points per serving: 6½
Total Points per recipe: 26

Variations:
Stir-fry 100 g (3½ oz) per person of chicken, prawns or beef along with the vegetables and then roll it all up in the tortillas. The Points per serving are: with chicken 8; with prawns 4½; with beef 10.
    Points per serving without guacamole are 5.

Seafood Pizza

Serves 4

Preparation and cooking time:
30 minutes + 30 minutes
proving
Calories per serving: 290

Freezing: not recommended

A luxurious pizza with a
deliciously crisp base.

For the pizza base:
175 g (6 oz) strong plain flour
7 g sachet of easy-blend dried
   yeast
a pinch of salt
2 teaspoons olive oil
For the tomato sauce:
1 onion, sliced finely
2 garlic cloves, crushed
1 teaspoon dried mixed herbs
400 g can of chopped tomatoes
2 tablespoons tomato purée
salt and freshly ground black
   pepper
For the topping:
200 g can of tuna in water,
   drained
125 g (4½ oz) packet of mixed
   seafood cocktail
2 tablespoons capers, drained
8 black olives
a handful of fresh basil leaves

Variations:
Substitute any of the following for the seafood topping to create
equally delicious pizzas but remember to count the Points.
   Gorgonzola and Pear – 3 tinned pear halves, sliced, 50 g (1¾ oz)
Gorgonzola cheese, crumbled. With the base, the Points will be
the same as the main recipe.
   Broccoli and Spicy Sausage – 100 g (3½ oz) blanched broccoli
florets, 50 g (1¾ oz) kabanos sausage, or 25 g (1 oz) sliced salami.
With the base, the Points will be the same as the main recipe.
   Vegetarian – 1 red pepper, de-seeded and sliced, 50 g (1¾ oz)
mushrooms, sliced, 50 g (1¾ oz) sweetcorn kernels, 50 g (1¾ oz)
half-fat mozzarella, grated. With the base, the Points will be 3½
per serving.

Weight Watchers note:
Pizzas can be high in fat and Calories since they tend to be topped
with lots of cheese. Making your own pizza not only allows you to
choose your own toppings, but also enables you to cut down on the
amount of cheese you use, if any.

Cook's note:
To save time, you could use a ready-made pizza base or even different
types of bread and then spread them with a store-bought tomato
pizza topping. Store-bought bases and toppings vary in Points, so
be sure to check the labels.

1. Preheat the oven to Gas Mark 6/200°C/400°F.
2. To make the pizza base, sift together the flour, yeast and salt. Stir
in half of the oil and 150 ml (¼ pint) hand-hot water. Mix to form
a soft dough, then knead on a lightly floured surface for 4–5 minutes,
or until smooth and elastic.
3. Place the dough in a clean, lightly oiled bowl. Cover with a damp
cloth and leave to prove in a warm place for 30 minutes or until
doubled in size.
4. Meanwhile, make the tomato sauce. Place all the ingredients in
a medium pan, bring to the boil and simmer gently for 10 minutes.
5. Remove the dough from the bowl and knead again on a lightly
floured surface for 4–5 minutes. Roll into a 25 cm (10-inch) round.
Place on a lightly oiled baking sheet, brush with a little oil and
spread over the tomato sauce.
6. Scatter over all the topping ingredients, drizzle over any remaining
oil and cook for 15–20 minutes on the floor of the oven, until the
dough is golden and crispy.

Points per serving: 4
Total Points per recipe: 16

Warm Bacon and Egg Salad

Serves 2

Preparation and cooking time:
20 minutes
Calories per serving: 210

Freezing: not recommended

This colourful and unusual
salad is so satisfying, it's a
meal in itself.

200 g (7 oz) baby new potatoes,
  scrubbed
2 rashers of smoked, lean back
  bacon
8 cherry tomatoes, halved
2 medium eggs
40 g (1½ oz) watercress
2 tablespoons fat-free
  vinaigrette
salt and freshly ground black
  pepper

1. Preheat the grill to high.
2. Cook the potatoes in boiling salted water until tender. Drain and
set aside.
3. Grill the bacon until crisp, then cut into pieces. Grill the tomatoes
for 1–2 minutes, or until cooked.
4. Meanwhile, bring a large pan of salted water to the boil and
reduce the heat to give a very gentle simmer. Break the eggs into
the water one at a time, gently stirring the water so the white
wraps around the yolk. Remove from the heat and leave to cook in
the water for 3 minutes. Remove with a slotted spoon.
5. Divide the watercress between 2 serving plates, top with the
bacon, tomatoes, potatoes and poached egg. Drizzle over the
vinaigrette. Season and serve immediately.

Points per serving: 3
Total Points per recipe: 6

Weight Watchers note:
Fat-free vinaigrettes are found in most supermarkets.

Mushroom Risotto

Serves 4

Preparation and cooking time:
30 minutes
Calories per serving: 345

Freezing: not recommended

Ⓥ if using vegetarian parmesan

This delicious, rich-tasting
dish may seem like it's full
of Calories but it isn't – the
risotto rice cleverly creates a
creamy flavour and texture as
it cooks.

1 teaspoon olive oil, corn oil or
  sunflower oil
1 garlic clove, crushed
1 small onion, chopped finely
350 g (12 oz) mushrooms (e.g.
  flat-cap, shiitake, oyster and
  button, sliced)
325 g (11½ oz) risotto or
  arborio rice
1.2 litres (2 pints) hot vegetable
  stock
40 g (1½ oz) parmesan, grated
2 tablespoons chopped fresh
  parsley
salt and freshly ground black
  pepper

1. Heat the oil in a large, heavy-based frying-pan over a medium
heat. Add the garlic, onion and mushrooms. Fry for 2 minutes.
2. Stir in the rice and cook for 1 minute, coating in the oil.
3. Add a ladleful of hot stock and allow the rice to absorb the liquid,
stirring continuously, before adding another ladleful. Continue in
this way until all the stock is used and the rice is cooked. (This
should take about 20 minutes in total.)
4. Stir in the parmesan and parsley, season and serve immediately.

Points per serving: 5½
Total Points per recipe: 22

Variations:
Omit the mushrooms and halfway through the cooking time in
step 3, stir in 225 g (8 oz) mixed spring vegetables such as asparagus,
fine beans and peas. The Points will be the same. Or when adding
the last ladleful of stock, stir in 100 g (3½ oz) halved cherry tomatoes,
4 chopped sun-dried tomatoes, 2 tablespoons sun-dried tomato
paste and 1 tablespoon chopped fresh rosemary. The Points will be
the same.

Cook's note:
Be aware that different types of risotto or arborio rice absorb different
amounts of liquid. When cooked, the rice should be tender but still
retain a little bit of bite.

Steak and Horseradish Baguette

Serves 1

Preparation and cooking time:
10 minutes
Calories per serving: 355

Freezing: not recommended

This sandwich is simple to make and full of flavour.

1 teaspoon oil
½ onion, sliced
100 g (3½ oz) flash-fry steak
15 cm (6-inch) piece of french baguette
2 teaspoons creamed horseradish sauce
1 tomato, sliced
a few lettuce leaves
salt and freshly ground black pepper

1. Heat the oil in a non-stick frying-pan, add the onion and fry for 2–3 minutes or until softened.
2. Push the onion to the side of the pan and add the steak. Fry for 1–2 minutes on each side. Remove from the heat.
3. Halve the bread lengthways, spread over the horseradish and then top with the onion, steak, tomato and lettuce. Season and serve immediately.

Points per serving: 9
Total Points per recipe: 9

Aubergine and Chick-pea Dahl

Serves 4

Preparation and cooking time:
20 minutes
Calories per serving: 345

Freezing: not recommended

Ⓥ

Serving warm pitta with dahl means you can enjoy mopping up all the lovely spicy sauce.

2 teaspoons oil
2 onions, chopped
2 aubergines (approximately 250 g/9 oz each), chopped
1½ teaspoons turmeric
1½ teaspoons cumin seeds
1½ teaspoons chilli powder
425 g can of chick-peas, drained and rinsed
400 g can of chopped tomatoes
2 tablespoons chopped fresh coriander
To serve:
4 medium pitta bread, warmed

1. Heat the oil in a non-stick frying pan, add the onions and aubergines and fry for 8–10 minutes, or until softened and golden.
2. Add the spices and continue to cook for 1 minute.
3. Add the remaining ingredients to the pan, bring to the boil, cover and simmer for 5 minutes and then stir through the coriander. Serve immediately with pitta bread.

Points per serving: 5
Total Points per recipe: 20

Tomato, Feta and Aubergine Roll-ups

Serves 2

Preparation and cooking time:
15 minutes
Calories per serving: 190

Freezing: not recommended

ⓥ if using vegetarian feta

Just another way to enjoy
wonderful Mediterranean
flavours.

1 aubergine, sliced lengthways
   into 6 slices (discard the
   ends and side strips)
1 tablespoon olive oil, corn oil
   or sunflower oil
40 g (1½ oz) feta cheese, sliced
6 sun-dried tomatoes, stored in
   oil, drained
12 fresh basil leaves
salt and freshly ground black
   pepper

1. Preheat the grill to high.
2. Brush each side of the aubergine slices with the oil and grill on
both sides until browned and softened. Remove from the grill.
3. Place a piece of feta, a sun-dried tomato and a couple of basil
leaves on each slice of aubergine. Season and roll up and secure
with a cocktail stick.
4. Place the aubergine rolls under the grill for 2–3 minutes, or
until the feta begins to melt.

Points per serving: 3
Total Points per recipe: 6

Cook's note:
These are also delicious cooked on the barbecue.

Variation:
If sun-dried tomatoes are unavailable, use slices of fresh tomato. You
could also use different herbs, such as rosemary or oregano.

Grilled Tuna Niçoise

Serves 2

Preparation and cooking time:
25 minutes
Calories per serving: 300

Freezing: not recommended

The texture of fresh tuna is
very different from the canned
variety and makes this classic
salad even better. It's a good
idea to try to eat oily fish,
such as tuna or mackerel,
once a week since this can
help to protect against heart
disease.

2 × 100 g (3½ oz) pieces of
   fresh tuna steak
juice of ½ lemon
175 g (6 oz) baby new potatoes,
   cooked
1 egg, hard-boiled, peeled and
   quartered
1 small red onion, cut into thin
   wedges
2 plum tomatoes, quartered
50 g (1¾ oz) cucumber, cubed
2 anchovies, halved (optional)
1 Little Gem lettuce, torn into
   bite-sized pieces
8 pitted black olives
25 g (1 oz) french beans,
   cooked and halved
2 tablespoons fat-free
   vinaigrette
salt and freshly ground black
   pepper

1. Preheat the grill to high.
2. Brush the tuna steaks with the lemon juice, season and then
place under the grill to cook for 7–8 minutes, turning halfway
through the cooking time.
3. In a large bowl, combine the remaining ingredients and divide
them between 2 plates. Top with the tuna steak.

Points per serving: 3½
Total Points per recipe: 7

Stuffed Baked Potato

Serves 1

Preparation time: 10 minutes
+ 1¾ hours cooking
Calories per serving: 185

Freezing: not recommended

Ⓥ if using vegetarian cheese

1 medium baking potato
25 g (1 oz) low-fat soft cheese
2 spring onions, sliced
1 tomato, chopped roughly
1 teaspoon whole-grain
    mustard

**Who could say no to a baked
potato? This one is creamy
and full of flavour.**

1. Preheat the oven to Gas Mark 6/200°C/400°F.
2. Prick the potato with a fork, then bake it for 1–1½ hours or
until tender.
3. Halve the potato and scoop out the filling and put into a bowl,
mash with a fork and then stir through all the remaining ingredients.
Season well, then spoon into the potato skins.
4. Return to the oven for 10–12 minutes or until the filling is
golden and bubbling.

Points per serving: 3
Total Points per recipe: 3

Weight Watchers note:
Potatoes make an ideal base for a meal since they are low in fat
and high in fibre. Try to choose fillings which are also low in fat,
such as lean ham, cottage cheese or baked beans, and remember
to count the Points.

Potato and Onion Omelette

Serves 1

Preparation and cooking time:
15 minutes
Calories per serving: 300

Freezing: not recommended

Ⓥ if using vegetarian Cheddar

**Omelettes are the ideal meal
for one. Serve with a simple
salad.**

2 eggs
1 tablespoon chopped fresh
    chives
½ teaspoon low-fat spread
1 medium potato, peeled,
    cooked and grated
1 small onion, chopped finely
15 g (½ oz) mature Cheddar,
    grated
salt and freshly ground black
    pepper

1. Whisk together the eggs, chives and 1 tablespoon of water.
Season well.
2. Melt the low-fat spread in a small non-stick frying-pan. Pour the
egg mixture into the pan. Using a wooden spatula, gently draw the
mixture into the middle of the pan as it sets, allowing the liquid
from the centre to run to the sides.
3. When the omelette has nearly set, spoon over the potato, onion
and cheese, season, and continue to cook for 30 seconds. Fold the
omelette in half, remove from the heat and allow to stand for
30 seconds.

Points per serving: 5
Total Points per recipe: 5

Variations:
Add 50 g (1¾ oz) cooked, peeled prawns and add 1 Point per serving.
You can also substitute 100 g (3½ oz) cooked vegetables for the
potato and deduct 1 Point per serving.

Picnics and Packed Lunches

Do you find that your lifestyle is so hectic that you are often grabbing lunch or dinner on the run? Well, Weight Watchers is coming to the rescue with these fast and simple ideas for packed lunches. Many of these recipes take 5, 10 or 15 minutes to prepare, so you can make them the night before or in the morning. Instead of all those fattening, ready-made sandwiches and take-away meals, you can now enjoy tasty, healthy lunches with dishes such as Lentil Salad or even some Honey, Ginger and Garlic Chicken Drumsticks.

Spiced Bean Pâté

Serves 4

Preparation and cooking time:
15 minutes
Calories per serving: 125

Freezing: recommended

Ⓥ

Serve this pâté with warm pitta bread for a tasty vegetarian option. Add 2¹/₂ Points per medium pitta.

1 tablespoon olive oil, corn oil
   or sunflower oil
1 onion, chopped
1 red chilli, chopped
1 garlic clove, crushed
1 teaspoon ground cumin
1 teaspoon ground coriander
1 teaspoon paprika
400 g can of black-eyed beans,
   drained and rinsed
2 tomatoes, chopped
2 tablespoons chopped fresh
   coriander

1. Heat the oil in a large non-stick frying-pan. Add the onion, chilli and garlic and fry for 2–3 minutes or until softened.
2. Add the cumin, coriander and paprika and continue to cook for 1 minute.
3. Stir in the beans and tomatoes and heat through.
4. Transfer to a food processor or blender and blend until almost smooth, but still retaining a little texture.
5. Stir in the coriander and serve.

Points per serving: 2¹/₂
Total Points per recipe: 10

Variations:
Try this pâté using different types of beans such as red kidney beans or a can of cooked green lentils.

Smoked Fish Pâté

Serves 4

Preparation time: 5 minutes
Calories per serving: 155

Freezing: recommended

Serve with raw vegetable sticks and crusty bread or crackers. Remember to add the extra Points.

150 g (5½ oz) peppered smoked mackerel fillets, skin removed
1 tablespoon lemon juice
125 g packet of low-fat soft cheese
1 tablespoon creamed horseradish sauce

1. Place all the ingredients in a food processor or blender and process for about 30 seconds until smooth, but still retaining a little texture.

Points per serving: 3½
Total Points per recipe: 14

Weight Watchers note:
Pâté is often high in fat and Calories. This recipe uses low-fat soft cheese which helps to keep down the Points.

Houmous

Serves 4

Preparation time: 10 minutes
Calories per serving: 120

Freezing: not recommended

Ⓥ

Houmous is a delicious and versatile Mediterranean treat – serve as a dip with pitta bread, adding the extra Points for the bread.

400 g can of chick-peas, drained and rinsed
grated rind and juice of 1 lemon
4 tablespoons light tahini paste
salt and freshly ground black pepper

1. Place the chick-peas in a food processor and blend until smooth.
2. Add the remaining ingredients and blend until well combined. Season to taste.

Points per serving: 3½
Total Points per recipe: 14

Weight Watchers note:
Store-bought houmous can be very high in fat since it contains a lot of oil. Look out for the reduced-fat varieties or, better still, make your own.

Variation:
Use houmous as a sandwich filling with lettuce leaves, grated carrot and plenty of freshly ground black pepper. The Points for the sandwich would be 5½ if using two medium slices of bread.

Spinach, Potato and Ricotta Parcels

Serves 4

Preparation and cooking time:
30–40 minutes
Calories per serving: 150

Freezing: not recommended

Ⓥ

Spinach, potato and ricotta
are a great combination and
taste wonderful wrapped up in
delicious filo pastry.

1 tablespoon olive oil, corn oil
    or sunflower oil
1 onion, chopped finely
1 garlic clove, crushed
1 medium potato, cooked,
    peeled and cut into 1 cm
    (1/2-inch) cubes
a pinch of nutmeg
150 g (51/2 oz) frozen chopped
    spinach
100 g (31/2 oz) ricotta
4 filo pastry sheets (25 cm/
    10 inches square)
salt and freshly ground black
    pepper

1. Preheat the oven to Gas Mark 6/200°C/400°F.
2. Heat 1 teaspoon of the oil in a non-stick frying-pan, add the
onion and garlic and fry for 2–3 minutes. Add the potato, nutmeg
and spinach and continue to cook for 4–5 minutes, or until all the
liquid from the spinach has evaporated.
3. Stir in the ricotta and season well.
4. Brush a sheet of filo with a little oil. Place another sheet of filo
on top and brush with oil. Repeat with the remaining two sheets
and cut each pile in half diagonally to create 4 filo triangles.
5. Divide the potato mixture into 4 and spoon onto the centre of
each of the 4 filo triangles.
6. Fold the ends of the pastry over the filling, forming a parcel
and enclosing the filling completely. Brush each parcel with the
remaining oil, place on a non-stick baking sheet and cook for
12–15 minutes or until golden.

Points per serving: 3
Total Points per recipe: 12

Weight Watchers note:
On a weight for weight basis, filo pastry is just as high in fat as
other types of pastry but you tend to use much less of it.

Herby Pasta Salad

Serves 4

Preparation and cooking time:
15 minutes
Calories per serving: 385

Freezing: not recommended

Ⓥ

A leafy green salad is ideal
with this refreshing pasta
dish.

350 g (12 oz) dried pasta shapes
150 g (51/2 oz) asparagus tips,
    or fine beans, halved
50 g (13/4 oz) frozen peas
3 tablespoons green pesto
1 tablespoon white wine
    vinegar
2 tablespoons capers, drained
2 tablespoons chopped fresh
    parsley
salt and freshly ground black
    pepper

1. Cook the pasta according to the packet instructions, adding the
asparagus (or beans) and peas 5 minutes before the end of cooking
time. Drain and transfer to a serving dish.
2. Mix together the remaining ingredients and immediately toss
through the pasta.
3. Leave the pasta to cool at room temperature and then serve.

Points per serving: 5
Total Points per recipe: 20

Wild Rice and Citrus Salad

Serves 4

Preparation and cooking time:
30 minutes
Calories per serving: 285

Freezing: not recommended

Ⓥ

Refreshing pieces of orange
tossed with rice make this a
delightful summer salad.
Serve with crusty bread.

200 g (7 oz) mixture of wild
 and long-grain rice
3 spring onions, sliced finely
1 orange, segmented and pith
 removed
1 yellow pepper, de-seeded and
 chopped
40 g (1½ oz) pine nuts, toasted
3 tablespoons fresh orange juice
1 tablespoon olive oil
3 tablespoons chopped fresh
 chives
salt and freshly ground black
 pepper

1. Cook the rice according to the packet instructions. Drain and
rinse under cold water.
2. Combine the remaining ingredients and toss through the rice.
Set aside for 10 minutes to allow the flavours to develop.

Points per serving: 4½
Total Points per recipe: 18

Cook's note:
Wild rice is sold in packets in most supermarkets.

Chicken, Apple and Watercress Salad

Serves 4

Preparation time: 10 minutes
Calories per serving: 200

Freezing: not recommended

A succulent chicken salad
tossed with a fat-free apple
dressing – quite refreshing!

2 medium ready-cooked
 skinless chicken breasts,
 sliced
100 g (3½ oz) watercress
2 eating apples, cored and
 chopped
50 g (1¾ oz) sultanas
40 g (1½ oz) walnuts, toasted
For the dressing:
4 tablespoons apple juice
1 teaspoon Dijon mustard
1 tablespoon white wine
 vinegar
1 teaspoon runny honey

1. Place all the ingredients for the dressing in a screw-top jar and
shake well to combine.
2. Toss together the salad ingredients, drizzle the dressing over the
salad and serve immediately.

Points per serving: 3½
Total Points per recipe: 14

Honey, Ginger and Garlic Chicken Drumsticks

Serves 4

Preparation time: 10 minutes
+ 30 minutes marinating
Cooking time: 20–25 minutes
Calories per serving: 115

Freezing: not recommended

This simple marinade really jazzes up chicken drumsticks.

4 chicken drumsticks, skin removed
2.5 cm (1-inch) fresh ginger, peeled and grated
1 garlic clove, crushed
1 tablespoon runny honey
2 tablespoons soy sauce
1 tablespoon dry sherry
1 teaspoon oil
1 tablespoon sesame seeds

1. Preheat the oven to Gas Mark 6/200°C/400°F.
2. Place the drumsticks in a non-metallic ovenproof dish.
3. Combine all the remaining ingredients, except the sesame seeds, and pour over the chicken. Leave to marinate for at least 30 minutes.
4. Cook the drumsticks for 15 minutes, basting occasionally. Sprinkle over the sesame seeds and continue to cook for 15 minutes or until the chicken is cooked through.

Points per serving: 2
Total Points per recipe: 8

Cook's note:
This recipe serves 2 as a main course and the Points per serving will be 4.

Lentil Salad

Serves 4

Preparation and cooking time:
15 minutes
Calories per serving: 150

Freezing: not recommended

Ⓥ

Enjoy this fragrant salad when it is still warm and at its best.

2 teaspoons olive oil
2 small red onions, cut into wedges
1 tablespoon chopped fresh rosemary or 1 teaspoon dried rosemary
4 plum tomatoes, quartered
2 × 400 g cans of green lentils, drained and rinsed
1 tablespoon garlic vinegar or white wine vinegar
salt and freshly ground black pepper

1. Heat the oil in a non-stick frying-pan. Add the onions and rosemary and fry for 4–5 minutes, or until the onions have softened and are beginning to brown. Add the tomatoes and continue to cook for 1 minute.
2. Stir through the lentils and vinegar, remove from the heat and season well.
3. Serve warm.

Points per serving: 3$\frac{1}{2}$
Total Points per recipe: 14

Cook's note:
If plum tomatoes are not available or are too expensive, use ordinary fresh tomatoes.

Tabbouleh

Serves 4

Preparation time: 10 minutes
+ 30 minutes soaking
Calories per serving: 230

Freezing: not recommended

Ⓥ

This refreshing Middle Eastern
salad traditionally accompanies
lamb dishes but you can also
enjoy it on its own.

250 g (9 oz) bulgar wheat
12 cherry tomatoes, quartered
100 g (3½ oz) cucumber,
   chopped finely
3 spring onions, sliced finely
3 tablespoons chopped fresh
   mint
3 tablespoons chopped fresh
   parsley
juice of 1 lemon
salt and freshly ground black
   pepper

1. Place the bulgar wheat in a large bowl and cover with plenty of
boiling water. Set aside for 30 minutes until tender, and then drain
off any excess liquid.
2. Toss together the remaining ingredients and stir in the bulgar
wheat.

Points per serving: 3½
Total Points per recipe: 14

Stuffed Rustic Loaf

Serves 4

Preparation time: 10 minutes
Calories per serving: 155

Freezing: not recommended

A welcome change from
traditional sandwiches. If you
want to take the loaf on a
picnic, simply tie it up with
string and carry in an airtight
container or wrapped in foil.
Cut it into wedges when ready
to serve.

1 small round rustic loaf
3 tablespoons fat-free
   vinaigrette
2 plum tomatoes, sliced
8 slices of Parma ham or lean
   cooked ham
12 pitted olives, halved
   lengthways
50 g (1¾ oz) cucumber, sliced
   thinly
50 g (1¾ oz) reduced-fat
   mozzarella, sliced thinly
60 g packet of rocket or lettuce
   leaves
3 spring onions, sliced
1 large carrot, grated
salt and freshly ground black
   pepper

1. Cut a 'lid' off the loaf, remove the inside of the bread and put
aside to use for breadcrumbs later. Drizzle half of the vinaigrette
into the bread cavity.
2. Layer the remaining ingredients into the loaf and drizzle over the
remaining vinaigrette. Season well and then replace the 'lid'.

Points per serving: 8
Total Points per recipe: 32

Cook's note:
Make the leftover bread into breadcrumbs and then use as you need
them. You can freeze them, if you wish.

Midweek Meals

The main meal is a good time to get all the family together, catch up on the news of the day and just enjoy each other's company. These are dishes which your family are sure to enjoy – and benefit from too! There'll be no more comments about diet food at the dinner table! Just lots of compliments and satisfied looks. If company's coming, there are plenty of wonderful ideas in this chapter, and since they don't take too long to make, you can actually enjoy the visit!

Fish Florentine

Serves 3

Preparation and cooking time:
30 minutes
Calories per serving: 240

Freezing: not recommended

An ideal supper dish which can be prepared in advance.

250 g (9 oz) fresh baby spinach or frozen spinach leaves
1 garlic clove, crushed
3 ripe tomatoes, sliced
250 g (9 oz) skinless cod fillet, cut into 3 equal pieces
For the cheese sauce:
25 g (1 oz) plain flour
300 ml (½ pint) skimmed milk
50 g (1¾ oz) Gruyère cheese, grated
salt and freshly ground black pepper

1. Preheat the oven to Gas Mark 6/200°C/400°F.
2. First make the cheese sauce. Place the flour in a non-stick saucepan and gradually stir in the milk. Place over a medium heat and bring to the boil, stirring continuously until the sauce has thickened. Season well and then stir in half of the Gruyère.
3. Place the spinach and garlic in a large non-stick pan over a medium heat and cook for 3–4 minutes, until the spinach has wilted and all the moisture has evaporated.
4. Place the tomatoes in the bottom of an ovenproof dish, layer over the spinach and then place the cod on top. Pour over the cheese sauce and then top with the other half of the cheese.
5. Cook for 15–20 minutes, until golden and bubbling.

Points per serving: 4
Total Points per recipe: 12

Weight Watchers note:
Combining flour and milk to make a white sauce means that no extra fat has to be used, which reduces the Points.

Spicy Cod Steaks

Serves 4

Preparation time: 15 minutes
+ 30 minutes marinating
Cooking time: 40 minutes
Calories per serving: 240

Freezing: not recommended

Cod steaks are wonderful with fragrant spices. Roasting the cumin seeds enhances their flavour, giving them a slightly nutty taste. However, if you do not have time, it's not essential.

4 thick skinless cod steaks (approximately 150 g/5¹/₂ oz) each)
1 teaspoon salt
¹/₂ teaspoon cayenne pepper
¹/₄ teaspoon turmeric
1 tablespoon vegetable oil
1 teaspoon fennel seeds
1 teaspoon black mustard seeds
1 onion, chopped finely
2 garlic cloves, crushed
1 large green chilli, de-seeded and chopped finely
1 red pepper, de-seeded and chopped
400 g can of chopped tomatoes
¹/₂ teaspoon ground cumin seeds, roasted if possible
a pinch of garam masala
2 tablespoons chopped fresh coriander

1. Pat the fish dry with kitchen paper. In a flameproof dish, mix together half of the salt, half of the cayenne pepper, turmeric and half of the oil. Place the fish in the dish and cover with the spice mixture. Leave to marinate for 30 minutes.
2. Heat the remaining ¹/₂ tablespoon of oil in a non-stick frying-pan and add the fennel seeds and mustard seeds. Fry until the mustard seeds start popping and then add the onion, garlic, chilli and red pepper. Fry for 5–6 minutes until the onion starts to brown.
3. Add the remaining salt and cayenne. Then add the tomatoes, cumin seeds and garam masala. Simmer for 15 minutes over a low heat.
4. Place the cod steaks under a preheated grill and grill on both sides for 3–4 minutes. Pour over the sauce, then cook in a preheated oven at Gas Mark 4/180°C/350°F for 15–20 minutes or until the fish is cooked. Serve with the coriander as a garnish.

Points per serving: 3
Total Points per recipe: 12

Cook's note:
All the spices listed in the ingredients list are available in supermarkets.
    To roast the cumin seeds, place them in a small pan and heat over a medium heat for 1–2 minutes until fragrant.

Trout Fillets with Orange, Caper and Spinach Sauce

Serves 4

Preparation and cooking time:
15 minutes
Calories per serving: 210

Freezing: not recommended

Orange juice enhances the delicate flavour of trout and the capers and baby spinach make it something special.

4 trout fillets, approximately 125 g (4¹/₂ oz) each
grated rind and juice of 2 oranges
2 tablespoons capers, drained
150 g (5¹/₂ oz) baby spinach
salt and freshly ground black pepper

1. Place the trout fillets in a medium non-stick frying-pan. Pour over the orange juice and rind and add the capers. Bring the juices to the boil and simmer gently for 4–5 minutes, or until the trout is cooked.
2. Add the spinach to the pan, gently stir into the sauce and allow to wilt. Season well and serve immediately.

Points per serving: 2
Total Points per recipe: 8

Chicken Stuffed with Olive and Lemon Tapenade

Serves 4

Preparation time: 10 minutes	4 medium boneless, skinless
Cooking time: 20–25 minutes	chicken breasts
Calories per serving: 190	100 g (3½ oz) pitted black
	olives
Freezing: not recommended	2 tablespoons capers, drained
	grated rind and juice of 1 lemon
Serve with boiled new potatoes	2 teaspoons olive oil
and a salad for a light summery	salt and freshly ground black
meal. Remember to add the	pepper
Points	

1. Preheat the oven to Gas Mark 6/200°C/400°F.
2. Make a horizontal slit along one side of each chicken breast to form a pocket.
3. In a food processor or blender, blend together the olives, capers, lemon rind and olive oil until combined but still retaining some texture. Season well.
4. Divide the olive paste between the chicken pockets and secure with a cocktail stick. Place the chicken in an ovenproof dish, pour over the lemon juice, cover with foil and cook for 20–25 minutes, or until cooked through.

Points per serving: 4
Total Points per recipe: 16

Weight Watchers note:
Olives add a lot of flavour to a meal without adding a lot of extra Points. 10 olives add just ½ Point.

Chicken with a Herb and Parmesan Crust

Serves 4

Preparation time: 10 minutes	4 medium boneless, skinless
Cooking time: 30–35 minutes	chicken breasts
Calories per serving: 265	4 tablespoons chicken stock
	2 tablespoons pesto
Freezing: not recommended	4 tablespoons fresh Granary®
	breadcrumbs
This dish is ideal as an	4 teaspoons grated parmesan
informal supper, served with	
fine beans and new potatoes.	
Remember to add the Points	
for the potatoes.	

1. Preheat the oven to Gas Mark 6/200°C/400°F.
2. Place the chicken breasts in a non-metallic ovenproof dish. Pour over the stock. Cover and cook for 20–25 minutes or until cooked through. Drain off the stock.
3. Mix together the pesto and half the breadcrumbs. Spoon this mixture over each chicken breast and press down with the back of a spoon. Combine the remaining breadcrumbs with the parmesan and sprinkle over the pesto-topped chicken, pressing down lightly.
4. Return the chicken to the oven and continue to cook for 8–10 minutes, or until the top is golden and bubbling.

Points per serving: 4½
Total Points per recipe: 18

Thai Vegetable Noodles with Chicken

Serves 4

Preparation and cooking time:
25 minutes + 30 minutes marinating
Calories per serving: 320

Freezing: not recommended

Thai food with its spicy, fragrant flavours has become increasingly popular over the last few years. If you love Thai food, this dish is sure to please.

4 teaspoons Thai red curry paste
grated rind and juice of 1 lime
2 teaspoons fish sauce or soy sauce
40 g (1½ oz) creamed coconut, dissolved in 6 tablespoons boiling water
2 medium boneless, skinless chicken breasts, sliced
1 teaspoon oil
1 red pepper, de-seeded and sliced
150 g (5½ oz) mangetout, halved
100 g (3½ oz) baby sweetcorn, halved lengthways
3 spring onions, sliced
250 g packet of rice noodles, cooked according to packet instructions
2 tablespoons chopped peanuts
2 tablespoons chopped fresh coriander

1. Mix together the curry paste, the rind and juice of the lime, the fish sauce or soy sauce and the creamed coconut in a medium bowl. Add the chicken and leave to marinate for at least 30 minutes.
2. Heat the oil in a large frying-pan or wok. Using a slotted spoon, add the chicken to the wok and fry for 3–4 minutes. Add the red pepper, mangetout and sweetcorn and continue to fry for 2–3 minutes. Toss in the spring onions, the marinade, the rice noodles, peanuts and coriander. Heat through and serve immediately.

Points per serving: 9
Total Points per recipe: 36

Variation:
For a vegetarian option, replace the chicken with 250 g (9 oz) tofu and cook the same way as the chicken. The Points will be 8½ per serving.

Minty Lamb Kebabs

Serves 4

Preparation and cooking time:
10 minutes + 30 minutes marinating
Calories per serving: 175

Freezing: not recommended

Nothing tastes better with lamb than mint, lemon and yogurt. Serve with warm pitta bread, salad and tomatoes.

2 garlic cloves, crushed
grated rind and juice of 1 lemon
1 teaspoon olive oil, corn oil or sunflower oil
2 tablespoons chopped fresh mint
2 tablespoons chopped fresh parsley
150 g (5½ oz) carton of low-fat natural yogurt
350 g (12 oz) lean lamb, cubed
2 small onions, cut into wedges
1 green pepper, de-seeded and cut into chunks
salt and freshly ground black pepper

1. Mix together the garlic, lemon rind and juice, oil, mint, parsley and yogurt.
2. Add the lamb, season, and leave to marinate for at least 30 minutes.
3. Thread the lamb on to 8 skewers, interspersing it with pieces of onion and pepper.
4. Cook on a barbecue or under a preheated grill for 8–10 minutes or until cooked through.

Points per serving: 4½
Total Points per recipe: 18

Lamb with Orange and Redcurrant Sauce

Serves 4

Preparation and cooking time:
15 minutes + 30 minutes marinating

Calories per serving: 195

Freezing: not recommended

Succulent lamb in fruity sauce is ideal for entertaining.

400 g (14 oz) lamb neck fillet, cut into 1 cm (1/2-inch) thick slices
2 garlic cloves, crushed
grated rind and juice of 2 medium oranges
2 sprigs of fresh rosemary
1 teaspoon olive oil, corn oil or sunflower oil
4 tablespoons redcurrant jelly
salt and freshly ground black pepper

1. Place the lamb in a non-metallic bowl and add the garlic, orange rind and juice and rosemary. Season well and marinate for at least 30 minutes.
2. Heat the oil in a non-stick frying-pan and, using a slotted spoon, add the lamb to the pan. Reserve the marinade.
3. Fry the lamb for 4–5 minutes or until browned on both sides. Pour over the reserved marinade, bring to the boil and simmer for 1 minute. Stir through the redcurrant jelly and heat through.

Points per serving: 7
Total Points per recipe: 28

Weight Watchers note:
Lamb can be high in fat so always make sure you choose lean cuts.

Cook's note:
If you prefer a slightly thicker sauce, stir a little arrowroot into the reserved juices in step 2.

Mixed Bean and Ratatouille Bake

Serves 4

Preparation time: 10 minutes
Cooking time: 35 minutes
Calories per serving: 255

Freezing: recommended

V if using vegetarian Cheddar

Ratatouille has the warm, luscious flavours of the south of France. Beans, pulses and a golden cheesy topping give this dish a nice twist.

1 teaspoon olive oil, corn oil or sunflower oil
1 large courgette, chopped
1 large aubergine, chopped
1 large onion, chopped
1 red pepper, de-seeded and chopped
1 green pepper, de-seeded and chopped
2 garlic cloves, crushed
12 pitted black olives, halved
400 g can of chopped tomatoes
1 tablespoon herbes de Provence or dried mixed herbs
400 g can of mixed pulses, drained and rinsed
150 g (5 1/2 oz) fine beans, halved
40 g (1 1/2 oz) mature Cheddar, grated finely
40 g (1 1/2 oz) ground almonds
3 tablespoons chopped fresh parsley
salt and freshly ground black pepper

1. Preheat the oven to Gas Mark 5/190°C/375°F.
2. Heat the oil in a large non-stick frying-pan. Add the courgette, aubergine, onion, red and green peppers and garlic. Fry for 5–6 minutes or until the vegetables are beginning to soften.
3. Add the olives, tomatoes, herbes de Provence, pulses and fine beans. Bring to the boil and simmer for 5 minutes. Season well and then transfer to an ovenproof dish.
4. Mix together the cheese, almonds and parsley and sprinkle over the vegetable mixture.
5. Bake in the oven for 25–30 minutes, or until golden and bubbling.

Points per serving: 4
Total Points per recipe: 16

Weight Watchers note:
Do not be tempted to add extra oil when frying the vegetables since they will add their delicious juices to the dish as they cook.

Peppers Stuffed with Pasta and Vegetables

Serves 2

Preparation time: 10 minutes
Cooking time: 30 minutes
Calories per serving: 260

Freezing: not recommended

Ⓥ if using vegetarian feta

Stuffed peppers are fun to make – even better to eat!

2 red peppers, halved and de-seeded
1 teaspoon olive oil, corn oil or sunflower oil
1 garlic clove, crushed
1 onion, chopped
1 courgette, chopped
1 teaspoon dried oregano
2 tablespoons pine nuts
40 g (1½ oz) feta cheese, crumbled
50 g (1¾ oz) small pasta shapes, cooked
1 tomato, chopped
salt and freshly ground black pepper

1. Preheat the oven to Gas Mark 6/200°C/400°F. Place the peppers, cut side upwards on a baking sheet.
2. Heat the oil in a non-stick frying-pan. Add the garlic, onion and courgette and fry for 4–5 minutes, or until softened.
3. Add the remaining ingredients to the frying-pan and stir through. Season well, then spoon the mixture into the pepper halves.
4. Cook for 20–25 minutes, or until the peppers are tender and the filling is golden. Serve immediately.

Points per serving: 4
Total Points per recipe: 8

Variation:
You could use cooked rice instead of pasta in this recipe. The Points would be the same.

Pasta with Tomato, Rosemary and Mushroom Sauce

Serves 4

Preparation and cooking time: 25 minutes
Calories per serving: 380

Freezing: not recommended

Ⓥ

Rosemary lends a distinctive flavour to this tasty pasta dish.

350 g (12 oz) dried pasta shapes
1 teaspoon olive oil, corn oil or sunflower oil
1 large onion, chopped finely
2 garlic cloves, crushed
100 g (3½ oz) button mushrooms, quartered
3 tablespoons sun-dried tomato paste
400 g can of chopped tomatoes
2 tablespoons chopped fresh rosemary or 1 teaspoon dried rosemary
100 g (3½ oz) ricotta cheese
salt and freshly ground black pepper

1. Cook the pasta according to the packet instructions.
2. Meanwhile, heat the oil in a non-stick frying-pan and add the onion, garlic and mushrooms. Fry for 3–4 minutes or until the onion is softened and the mushrooms are cooked.
3. Add the sun-dried tomato paste, chopped tomatoes and rosemary to the onion mixture, bring to the boil, cover and simmer for 5 minutes. Stir in the ricotta and season.
4. Drain the pasta, stir through the sauce and serve immediately.

Points per serving: 5
Total Points per recipe: 20

Pork with Prune and Apricot Couscous

Serves 4

Preparation and cooking time:
30 minutes
Calories per serving: 360

Freezing: not recommended

**Mildly spiced couscous is
ideal with pork tenderloin.**

2 teaspoons olive oil, corn oil
   or sunflower oil
1 onion, chopped
1 teaspoon ground cumin
1 teaspoon ground coriander
1/2 teaspoon chilli powder
600 ml (1 pint) vegetable stock
250 g (9 oz) couscous
350 g (12 oz) pork tenderloin,
   sliced
50 g (1 3/4 oz) ready-to-eat dried
   prunes, chopped
50 g (1 3/4 oz) ready-to-eat dried
   apricots, chopped
2 tablespoons chopped fresh
   coriander

1. Heat half of the oil in a non-stick frying-pan, add the onion and fry for 3–4 minutes, until softened. Stir in the spices and continue to cook for 1 minute.
2. In a separate pan, bring the vegetable stock to the boil, remove from the heat and add the couscous. Cover and set aside for 5 minutes or until tender. Fluff up the couscous with a fork to remove any lumps.
3. Heat the remaining oil in a pan and fry the pork for 3–4 minutes on each side, or until browned and cooked through.
4. Stir the couscous, prunes, apricots and coriander together with the onion and spice mixture. Serve alongside the pork.

Points per serving: 7
Total Points per recipe: 28

Variation:
Replace the couscous with soaked bulgar wheat for a tasty alternative. Deduct 1/2 Point per serving.

Pork with Mushroom, Mustard and Tarragon Sauce

Serves 4

Preparation and cooking time:
20 minutes
Calories per serving: 275

Freezing: not recommended

**This pork dish in a light
creamy sauce is delicious
served with steamed leeks and
potatoes.**

2 teaspoons olive oil, corn oil
   or sunflower oil
4 medium lean pork steaks
1 onion, chopped finely
250 g (9 oz) mixed mushrooms
   (e.g. chestnut, oyster, open-
   cap), sliced
4 tablespoons dry white wine or
   vegetable stock
1 tablespoon whole-grain
   mustard
125 ml (4 fl oz) half-fat crème
   fraîche
2 tablespoons chopped fresh
   tarragon or 1 teaspoon dried
   tarragon
salt and freshly ground black
   pepper

1. Heat the oil in a non-stick frying-pan. Fry the pork steaks for 3–4 minutes on each side or until browned and cooked through. Remove from the pan with a slotted spoon and keep warm.
2. Add the onion and mushrooms to the pan and fry for 3–4 minutes or until softened. Pour over the wine or stock, allow to bubble and reduce by half. Stir in the mustard, crème fraîche and tarragon. Season well.
3. Return the pork steaks to the pan, along with any juices. Bring to the boil, simmer for 1 minute, then serve.

Points per serving: 6 1/2
Total Points per recipe: 26

Weight Watchers note:
Light crème fraîche contains about half the Calories of double cream.

Delicious Desserts

Don't think that desserts are a thing of the past now that you're dieting. If you are counting the Points, you can enjoy the food you love and still lose weight. Many of these recipes include fruit, which is low in Calories and Points, but is an absolute taste sensation. Sorbets, strawberries in foil parcels with mint and rosewater, hot baked bananas with honey, lemon and almonds and caramelised apples are just some of the irresistible delights in this chapter. And most are ready in minutes.

Mixed Berry Sorbet

Serves 6

Preparation time: 15 minutes + freezing
Calories per serving: 135

Ⓥ if using free-range eggs

Sorbets are wonderfully refreshing – they're the perfect way to end a meal.

750 g (1 lb 10 oz) mixed summer berries (e.g. strawberries, blackberries, raspberries)
150 g (5½ oz) caster sugar
1 tablespoon lemon juice
2 egg whites

1. Place the fruit in a blender or food processor and blend until smooth.
2. Place the sugar, 125 ml (4 fl oz) water and the lemon juice in a medium pan and heat gently until the sugar has dissolved. Bring to the boil and simmer for 3 minutes. Remove from the heat and cool.
3. Add the cooled sugar and water mixture to the blender with the fruit and process for 10 seconds.
4. Pour the mixture through a nylon sieve to remove any pips. Transfer the strained mixture to a plastic freezer-proof container.
5. Meanwhile, whisk the egg whites until they form soft peaks. Fold into the berry mixture and then place in the freezer.
6. After 1 hour, remove the sorbet from the freezer and beat with a fork to remove any ice crystals. Return to the freezer.
7. After a further hour, beat the sorbet again and then leave to freeze completely.

Points per serving: 2
Total Points per recipe: 12

Variations:
Feel free to use different fruits, such as redcurrants and blueberries.

Hot Strawberry Parcels

Serves 4

Preparation and cooking time:
20 minutes
Calories per serving: 65

Freezing: not recommended

(V)

These strawberries are
beautifully fragrant and such a
treat when served hot with
crème fraîche.

350 g (12 oz) fresh
  strawberries, hulled and
  halved
1 tablespoon chopped fresh
  mint
1 tablespoon rosewater
1 tablespoon caster sugar
To serve:
4 tablespoons half-fat crème
  fraîche
a few drops of vanilla essence

1. Preheat the oven to Gas Mark 6/200°C/400°F.
2. Cut out four pieces of foil, each approximately 25 cm/10 inches
square.
3. Divide the strawberries between the pieces of foil. Bring the
edges of the foil up slightly, sprinkle over the mint, rosewater and
caster sugar and seal the parcels.
4. Place the parcels on a baking sheet and cook for 10–15 minutes
or until the fruits are softened.
5. Mix together the crème fraîche and vanilla essence and serve
with the hot strawberries, turned out of the foil.

Points per serving: 1½
Total Points per recipe: 6

Cook's note:
Rosewater is usually available from large chemists and supermarkets.

Melon Delight

Serves 6

Preparation time: 15 minutes
+ freezing
Calories per serving: 130

(V)

This refreshing and sparkly
dessert is ideal for a summer
dinner party.

1 cantaloupe melon, peeled,
  de-seeded and chopped
150 g (5½ oz) caster sugar
2 tablespoons rosewater

1. Place the melon in a food processor or blender and process until
smooth.
2. Add the sugar to the blender and process for 10 seconds.
3. Pour in 600 ml (1 pint) of water and the rosewater and process
until well combined.
4. Strain the liquid through a nylon sieve into a plastic freezer
container and freeze for 2 hours.
5. Remove the melon mixture from the freezer and beat with a
fork. Return to the freezer. Repeat this process twice at 1-hourly
intervals. When ready, the mixture should look like shattered glass.
If not, freeze for longer.

Points per serving: 2
Total Points per recipe: 12

Variations:
For a change, you could use watermelon.

59

Baked Bananas

Serves 4

Preparation and cooking time: 20 minutes

Calories per serving: 175

Freezing: not recommended

Ⓥ

4 medium bananas, cut into chunks
4 tablespoons blossom honey, or runny honey
grated rind and juice of 1 lemon
To serve:
40 g (1½ oz) toasted flaked almonds

Cooking bananas intensifies their flavour.

1. Preheat the oven to Gas Mark 6/200°C/400°F.
2. Divide the banana between 4 squares of foil large enough to cover the bananas. Drizzle over the honey and lemon rind and juice and then wrap up the parcels.
3. Bake for 12–15 minutes or until the banana is tender. Serve sprinkled with the almonds.

Points per serving: 4
Total Points per recipe: 16

Cook's note:
These banana parcels can also be cooked on the barbecue.

Stewed Prunes with Brandy

Serves 4

Preparation and cooking time: 5 minutes + overnight soaking

Calories per serving: 150

Freezing: not recommended

Ⓥ

350 g (12 oz) pitted ready-to-eat prunes
4 tablespoons brandy
To serve:
2 tablespoons half-fat crème fraîche

Brandy and prunes are a wonderful combination and just perfect for a treat in the bleak midwinter.

1. Place the prunes and 200 ml (7 fl oz) of water in a pan. Bring to the boil and simmer for 1 minute. Remove from the heat and transfer to a bowl.
2. Stir through the brandy, cover and refrigerate overnight.
3. Serve with the crème fraîche.

Points per serving: 2½
Total Points per recipe: 10

Variations:
Place the prunes in a pan with 200 ml (7 fl oz) strong black tea and a cinnamon stick. Simmer for 1 minute and then leave to soak overnight.

Try using a variety of dried fruits, such as apricots, figs and apples.

Caramelised Apples with Toasted Raisin Bread

Serves 2

Preparation and cooking time:
20 minutes
Calories per serving: 250

Freezing: not recommended

Ⓥ

Apples are so wonderful when they are caramelised and toasted raisin bread is the perfect partner for them.

grated rind and juice of 1 lemon
25 g (1 oz) light soft brown
  sugar
25 g (1 oz) butter
1/2 teaspoon ground cinnamon
3 eating apples, cored and
  sliced
4 small slices of raisin bread

1. Place the lemon juice and rind, brown sugar, butter and cinnamon in a non-stick frying-pan. Heat gently until the sugar has dissolved.
2. Add the apples to the pan and cook over a low heat for 5–6 minutes or until beginning to caramelise, turning occasionally.
3. Meanwhile, toast the raisin bread under a preheated grill.
4. Spoon the caramelised apples over the raisin bread and serve.

Points per serving: 6 1/2
Total Points per recipe: 13

Variation:
Pears are an excellent substitute for apples in this recipe. Add 1 Point per serving.

Hot Tropical Fruit Salad

Serves 3

Preparation and cooking time:
10 minutes
Calories per serving: 120

Freezing: not recommended

Ⓥ

This simple dessert brings you a taste of the tropics.

432 g can of pineapple chunks
  in juice, drained and juice
  reserved
grated rind and juice of 1 lemon
2 pieces of preserved ginger
  in syrup, chopped, plus 2
  tablespoons of the syrup
1 mango, peeled and chopped
2 kiwi fruit, peeled and sliced
1 medium banana, chopped
To serve:
3 tablespoons Greek-style
  natural yogurt

1. Place the pineapple juice, lemon rind and juice, ginger and ginger syrup in a medium pan.
2. Bring to the boil and add the pineapple chunks, mango, kiwi and banana.
3. Heat through and serve topped with a tablespoon of Greek-style natural yogurt.

Points per serving: 4
Total Points per recipe: 12

Cook's note:
This is also delicious served chilled with a little vanilla ice-cream. Remember to add the extra Points.

Raspberry Cheesecake

Serves 8

Preparation time: 30 minutes
+ 3 hours chilling
Calories per serving: 200

Freezing: not recommended

Ⓥ

This light and fruity cheesecake
is a delightful treat.

For the base:
200 g (7 oz) digestive biscuits,
   crushed
50 g (1³/₄ oz) butter, melted

For the topping:
1 sachet of raspberry sugar-free
   jelly
450 g (1 lb) fresh raspberries, or
   frozen raspberries, defrosted
200 g (7 oz) very-low-fat plain
   fromage frais
25 g (1 oz) caster sugar

1. Mix together the biscuits and butter and press into a lined loose-bottomed 20 cm (8-inch) deep cake tin. Refrigerate for at least 30 minutes or until the base has set.

2. Add enough boiling water to the jelly crystals to make 300 ml (¹/₂ pint) of jelly. Leave to cool.

3. Purée half of the raspberries in a food processor or blender. Pass through a fine nylon sieve to remove any pips. Stir the purée, whole raspberries, fromage frais and caster sugar through the cooled jelly and pour over the biscuit base. Chill for 2–3 hours or until set. Garnish with a few extra raspberries.

Points per serving: 4¹/₂
Total Points per recipe: 36

Weight Watchers note:
Traditional cheesecakes tend to be high in fat since they contain a lot of cream. Using fromage frais helps to cut down on the Points.

Lemon Meringue Frozen Yogurt

Serves 6

Preparation time: 5 minutes + freezing
Calories per serving: 145

Ⓥ

6 tablespoons luxury lemon curd
500 g (1 lb 2 oz) Greek-style natural yogurt
150 g (5½ oz) very-low-fat plain fromage frais
grated rind and juice of 1 lemon
2 meringue nests, crushed lightly

1. Mix together the lemon curd, yogurt, fromage frais, lemon rind and juice.
2. Pour into a freezer-proof plastic container and freeze for 2 hours. Beat with a fork to remove any ice crystals.
3. Stir in the meringue, return to the freezer and freeze until firm.

Points per serving: 3½
Total Points per recipe: 21

Variation:
Use orange curd in place of the lemon curd.

Mocha 'n' Orange Mousse

Serves 6

Preparation time: 20 minutes + 1 hour chilling
Calories per serving: 230

Freezing: not recommended

Ⓥ

The flavours of chocolate and orange make this mousse irresistible!

100 g (3½ oz) plain chocolate, broken into squares
1 tablespoon instant coffee, dissolved in 1 tablespoon boiling water
grated rind of 2 oranges
2 oranges, pith removed, and flesh chopped
150 ml (¼ pint) whipping cream
25 g (1 oz) caster sugar
300 g (½ pint) low-fat plain fromage frais

1. Place the chocolate and dissolved coffee in a bowl over a pan of simmering water. Heat until melted, stir in the orange rind and flesh. Leave to cool.
2. Meanwhile, whip the cream and the sugar until soft peaks form. Fold in the fromage frais, stir in the chocolate mixture and spoon into 4 ramekins. Chill until firm.

Points per serving: 5½
Total Points per recipe: 33

Cherry Crisp

Serves 4

Preparation and cooking time:
25 minutes
Calories per serving: 175

Freezing: not recommended

Ⓥ

Enjoy the succulence of
cherries under this crisp
nutty topping.

250 g (9 oz) fresh or canned
 cherries, stoned
1 tablespoon caster sugar
2 tablespoons water
For the topping:
50 g (1³/₄ oz) rolled oats
25 g (1 oz) demerara sugar
15 g (¹/₂ oz) flaked almonds
1 tablespoon sesame seeds
1 tablespoon runny honey

1. Preheat the oven to Gas Mark 6/200°C/400°F.
2. Place the cherries in an ovenproof dish, sprinkle over the sugar
and water, then cook for 10 minutes or until beginning to soften.
3. Meanwhile, mix together all the ingredients for the topping.
Sprinkle this mixture over the cherries and return to the oven for
10–12 minutes or until crisp and golden.

Points per serving: 3
Total Points per recipe: 12

Variations:
A variety of fruits, such as plums or blackberries, can be used in
this pudding with equally delicious results.

Fruit Fool

Serves 4

Preparation time: 10 minutes
Calories per serving: 130

Freezing: not recommended

Ⓥ

An inexpensive, easy and
versatile dish – keep it in
mind when you have
unexpected guests and need
to whip up a dessert.

200 ml (7 fl oz) light evaporated
 milk, chilled
1 tablespoon caster sugar
350 g (12 oz) mixed fresh
 berries (e.g. strawberries,
 raspberries, blueberries)

1. Pour the evaporated milk into a large bowl and whisk until
thickened and doubled in volume. Stir in the sugar.
2. Lightly crush two-thirds of the fruit and add to the evaporated milk.
3. Spoon into 4 glass serving dishes and decorate with the
remaining fruit.

Points per serving: 2¹/₂
Total Points per recipe: 10

Cook's note:
Serve this dessert within 30 minutes of making it, otherwise it may
start to go watery.

Home Baking

What could be more comforting or inviting than the aroma of freshly baked bread, cakes and biscuits? And what could be more of a problem for dieters! Well, there's no more need to worry with these recipes from Weight Watchers. Banish the thought of not having a few treats and enjoy muffins, teacakes, loaves and biscuits with your cup of tea – just remember to count the Points.

Parmesan and Herb Rolls

Serves 8

Preparation time: 20 minutes + 1 hour proving
Cooking time: 20 minutes
Calories per serving: 240

Freezing: recommended

Ⓥ if using vegetarian parmesan

Nothing beats the taste and aroma of freshly baked bread.

450 g (1 lb) strong wholemeal flour
1 teaspoon salt
7 g sachet of easy-blend dried yeast
25 g (1 oz) polyunsaturated margarine
50 g (1¾ oz) grated parmesan
6 tablespoons chopped fresh parsley
3 spring onions, sliced
a little milk, for brushing

1. In a large bowl, mix together the flour, salt and yeast.
2. Rub in the margarine, using your fingertips. Add the parmesan, parsley and spring onions and stir through.
3. Pour over 300 ml (½ pint) hand-hot water and, using your hands, mix in the water and form a soft dough.
4. Tip the dough onto a lightly floured surface and knead for 8 minutes, until smooth and elastic. Place in a lightly-oiled clean bowl, cover with a damp cloth and leave to prove in a warm place until doubled in size.
5. Re-knead the dough for a further 5 minutes. Divide the dough into 8 pieces and knead each to form a roll. Place the rolls on a baking sheet and then cover and leave to prove again, until almost doubled in size again. Preheat the oven to Gas Mark 6/200°C/400°F.
6. Brush with a little milk and then bake for 20 minutes or until the rolls are golden and sound hollow when tapped.

Points per serving: 4
Total Points per recipe: 32

Honey and Sunflower Bread

Serves 12

Preparation and cooking time: 20 minutes + 1 hour proving
Calories per serving: 195

Freezing: recommended

Ⓥ

This nutty bread is ideal for sandwiches and tastes even better when toasted.

450 g (1 lb) Granary® flour
1 teaspoon salt
7 g sachet of easy-blend dried yeast
25 g (1 oz) sesame seeds
75 g (2¾ oz) sunflower seeds
2 tablespoons honey

1. In a large bowl, mix together the flour, salt, yeast, sesame seeds and all but 1 tablespoon of sunflower seeds.
2. Stir half of the honey into 250 ml (9 fl oz) of hand-hot water, pour into the bowl with the flour mixture and combine to form a soft dough.
3. Tip the dough on to a lightly floured surface and knead for 8 minutes, until smooth.
4. Place the dough into a lightly-oiled bowl, cover with a damp cloth and leave to prove in a warm place, until doubled in size.
5. Re-knead the dough for 5 minutes, then transfer to a lightly-oiled and floured 900 g (2 lb) loaf tin. Leave to prove again until almost doubled in size again. Preheat the oven to Gas Mark 6/200°C/400°F. Brush with the remaining honey and sprinkle over the remaining sunflower seeds. Bake for 30–35 minutes or until golden and hollow when tapped.

Points per serving: 2½
Total Points per recipe: 30

Apricot and Cinnamon Muffins

Serves 8

Preparation time: 15 minutes
Cooking time: 12 minutes
Calories per serving: 150

Freezing: recommended

Ⓥ if using a free-range egg

Light and airy, these tasty
muffins are also low in Points.

75 g (2¾ oz) plain flour
75 g (2¾ oz) wholemeal plain
  flour
2 teaspoons baking powder
1 teaspoon ground cinnamon
1 egg, beaten
25 g (1 oz) caster sugar
125 ml (4½ fl oz) semi-
  skimmed milk
50 g (1¾ oz) polyunsaturated
  margarine, melted
½ teaspoon vanilla essence
50 g (1¾ oz) ready-to-eat dried
  apricots, chopped

1. Preheat the oven to Gas Mark 6/200°C/400°F.
2. Sift the flours, baking powder and cinnamon together onto a large
sheet of greaseproof paper to make the muffins light and airy.
3. In a large bowl, mix together the egg, sugar, milk, margarine and
vanilla essence.
4. Sift the dry ingredients into the bowl and stir gently. Add the
apricots and combine lightly.
5. Spoon the mixture into 8 paper muffin cases and then place in a
muffin tray. Bake for 10–12 minutes or until golden and risen.

Points per serving: 2½
Total Points per recipe: 20

Cook's note:
Don't be tempted to beat the mixture. It is actually the lumpy
consistency of the mixture which helps to make the muffins light
and airy.

Variations:
Use different fruits to suit your taste, such as sultanas and
chopped dates.

Lemon, Lime and Honey Cake

Serves 8

Garnish with grated lemon and
lime peel for a pretty effect.

Preparation time: 20 minutes
Cooking time: 25 minutes
Calories per serving: 110

Freezing: recommended

Ⓥ if using free-range eggs

Perfect with a cup of tea.

3 eggs, separated
2 tablespoons caster sugar
3 tablespoons runny honey
grated rind of 1 lemon
grated rind of 1 lime
50 g (1¾ oz) cornflour, sifted
100 g (3½ oz) self-raising flour,
  sifted
For the icing:
50 g (1¾ oz) icing sugar
2 teaspoons lemon or lime juice

1. Preheat the oven to Gas Mark 6/200°C/400°F.
2. In a large bowl, beat together the egg yolks, sugar, honey and the
lemon and lime rind.
3. Whisk the egg whites until they form soft peaks, then fold into
the other mixture, along with the cornflour and flour.
4. Spoon the mixture into a lightly greased and lined 20 cm (8-inch)
loose-bottomed cake tin. Bake for 20–25 minutes or until firm to
the touch.
5. Turn on to a wire rack and leave to cool.
6. Mix together the icing sugar and lemon or lime juice and spread
over the cooled cake.

Points per serving: 3
Total Points per recipe: 24

Blackberry and Apple Cake

Serves 10

Preparation time: 20 minutes
Cooking time: 45 minutes –
1 hour
Calories per serving: 185

Freezing: recommended

Ⓥ if using free-range eggs

Juicy autumn fruits give this
cake a lovely, moist texture.

150 g (5½ oz) self-raising flour
2 teaspoons baking powder
75 g (2¾ oz) polyunsaturated
   margarine
50 g (1¾ oz) ground almonds
75 g (2¾ oz) caster sugar
2 eggs
6 tablespoons apple juice
a few drops of vanilla essence
1 cooking apple, peeled, cored
   and chopped
100 g (3½ oz) blackberries
1 tablespoon demerara sugar

1. Preheat the oven to Gas Mark 6/200°C/400°F.
2. In a large bowl, beat together the flour, baking powder, margarine,
ground almonds, caster sugar, eggs, apple juice and vanilla essence.
3. Fold in the apple and blackberries and spoon the mixture into a
lightly greased and lined 20 cm (8-inch) loose-bottomed cake tin.
Sprinkle over the demerara sugar and bake for 45 minutes – 1 hour,
or until golden and firm to the touch.
4. Turn out on to a wire rack and leave to cool.

Points per serving: 3½
Total Points per recipe: 35

Variations:
Raspberries and pears also work well as a combination in this cake.

Orange and Sesame Cake

Serves 8

Preparation time: 20 minutes
Cooking time: 30 minutes
Calories per serving: 200

Freezing: recommended

Ⓥ if using free-range eggs

75 g (2¾ oz) butter
100 g (3½ oz) caster sugar
100 g (3½ oz) self-raising flour
1 teaspoon baking powder
2 eggs, separated
grated rind and juice of 1 orange
25 g (1 oz) sesame seeds,
    toasted

Toasted sesame seeds give this cake an unusual nutty flavour.

1. Preheat the oven to Gas Mark 6/200°C/400°F.
2. In a large bowl, beat together the butter and sugar until light and fluffy. Stir in 1 tablespoon of the flour and the baking powder and then gradually beat in the egg yolks.
3. Stir in the remaining flour, the orange rind and juice and the sesame seeds.
4. Meanwhile, whisk the egg whites until they form soft peaks and then stir into the cake mixture.
5. Spoon into a lightly greased and lined 20 cm (8-inch) loose-bottomed cake tin. Bake for 25–30 minutes or until golden and firm to the touch.
6. Transfer to a wire rack and leave to cool.

Points per serving: 4½
Total Points per recipe: 36

Banana and Pecan Loaf

Serves 14

Preparation time: 20 minutes
Cooking time: 1 hour
Calories per serving: 175

Freezing: recommended

Ⓥ if using a free-range egg

175 g (6 oz) dried stoned dates
1 egg
2 tablespoons runny honey
100 g (3½ oz) pecan nuts,
    chopped
450 g (1 lb) ripe bananas,
    peeled and mashed roughly
225 g (8 oz) wholemeal flour

Have this loaf on hand for when friends drop by.

1. Preheat the oven to Gas Mark 4/180°C/350°F.
2. Place the dates and 125 ml (4½ fl oz) of water in a medium pan and simmer gently until the dates are soft and pulpy. Remove from the heat, transfer to a large bowl and leave to cool for 10 minutes. Then beat in the egg, honey, nuts and mashed bananas.
3. Sift the flour into the date mixture and combine thoroughly. Spoon into a greased and lined 900 g (2 lb) loaf tin and make the surface smooth.
4. Bake for 1 hour or until a skewer comes out clean when inserted into the middle.
5. Leave to cool in the tin for 15 minutes and then transfer to a wire rack to cool completely.

Points per serving: 3
Total Points per recipe: 42

Weight Watchers note:
Making a purée with dates means that no added fat is needed in the cake.

Fruit and Nut Bars

Serves 6

Preparation time: 10 minutes
Cooking time: 15 minutes
Calories per serving: 210

Freezing: recommended

Ⓥ

These tasty bars never go out of style – why not take them on a picnic, slip them into a lunchbox or share them with friends?

50 g (1³/₄ oz) polyunsaturated margarine
2 tablespoons golden syrup
25 g (1 oz) muscovado sugar
75 g (2³/₄ oz) rolled oats
50 g (1³/₄ oz) self-raising flour
25 g (1 oz) mixed nuts, chopped roughly
50 g (1³/₄ oz) dried fruit (e.g. apricots, dates, sultanas)
2 tablespoons sunflower seeds

1. Preheat the oven to Gas Mark 4/180°C/350°F.
2. Place the margarine, syrup and sugar in a medium pan and warm over a low heat until the margarine has melted and the sugar has dissolved.
3. Stir in the remaining ingredients and press into a 15 cm (6-inch) square non-stick baking tin.
4. Place in the oven and cook for 12–15 minutes or until golden.
5. Cut into 6 bars, leave to cool slightly and then transfer to a wire baking tray to cool.

Points per serving: 4
Total Points per recipe: 24

Polenta and Almond Biscuits

Serves 18

Preparation time: 10 minutes
+ 30 minutes chilling
Cooking time: 7–8 minutes
Calories per serving: 70

Freezing: not recommended

Ⓥ if using a free-range egg

Polenta gives these delicious biscuits an added nutty crunch.

75 g (2³/₄ oz) polenta
40 g (1¹/₂ oz) plain flour
¹/₂ teaspoon baking powder
75 g (2³/₄ oz) icing sugar
50 g (1³/₄ oz) butter
1 teaspoon almond essence
1 egg yolk
25 g (1 oz) flaked almonds

1. Put the polenta, flour, baking powder and sugar in a large bowl. Rub in the butter using your fingertips.
2. Stir in the almond essence and egg yolk and combine to form a soft dough. Wrap the dough in clingfilm and refrigerate for 30 minutes. Preheat the oven to Gas Mark 4/180°C/350°F.
3. Roll out the dough on a lightly floured surface to a thickness of 3 mm (¹/₈ inch). Using a 4 cm (2¹/₂-inch) round cutter, cut the dough into biscuits. Transfer the biscuits to a baking sheet, covered in baking parchment, and sprinkle over the flaked almonds. Bake for 7–8 minutes or until golden.
4. Cool on a wire rack.

Points per serving: 1¹/₂
Total Points per recipe: 27

Cook's note:
Polenta is a very fine Italian cornmeal which is now sold in packets in most supermarkets. Buy the polenta in grains – not the ready-made sort – for this recipe.

Index